6CR→

*R01144 45

D1209541

THE ODES OF KEATS

THE ODES OF KEATS

AND THEIR EARLIEST KNOWN

MANUSCRIPTS

Introduced with notes by

Robert Gittings

John Keats

THE KENT STATE
UNIVERSITY PRESS

Devised, designed and produced by Ruari McLean Associates, London
The text printed in Great Britain at
The Curwen Press, Plaistow, London E13
The plates printed offset-litho in the United States of America
by Meriden Gravure Company, Meriden, Connecticut
Bound in Great Britain by the Wigmore Bindery, London
Simultaneously published in the United Kingdom
by Heinemann Educational Books Ltd

Standard Book Number 87338-099-1
Library of Congress Catalog Card Number 70-109442

ACKNOWLEDGEMENTS

The author gratefully acknowledges assistance from Mary A. Benjamin, William H. Bond, Amy Lady Coats, P. J. Croft, Frances Hamill, Lola L. Szladits, Robert H. Taylor, and Alfred W. Van Sinderen, in preparing his text. Thanks are also due to all the libraries concerned, for their willing co-operation.
The portrait of Keats on the title-page is reproduced from the drawing by Joseph Severn in the Victoria and Albert Museum.

Published by
The Kent State University Press, Ohio

CONTENTS

HOW THE ODES WERE
WRITTEN
APRIL TO SEPTEMBER 1819

In his volume, *Lamia, Isabella, The Eve of St Agnes, and other poems*, published at the end of June 1820, John Keats included, among these other poems, five Odes. Four of these had been written the previous summer, together with a fifth, *On Indolence*; but when preparing his poems to show his publishers in autumn 1819, he had rejected *Indolence*, and, the mood of the summer revived by re-reading the others, he had composed and substituted the supreme *To Autumn*. That this is not actually called an ode in the 1820 volume is due, it has been convincingly shown by H. W. Garrod, to an error by Keats's publishers; Keats himself never gave it any title, but its style and nature show that his mind during composition was working in the framework he had devised for himself in the summer odes.

The five poems actually published can therefore be considered as a whole; and, in fact, consideration of them has generally led to the conclusion that they are Keats's masterpieces. There is a danger here, however, in regarding them as the culmination of Keats's work; and, particularly with *To Autumn*, as summing-up all he had to say. The Odes, like everything else he wrote, represent distinct and separable stages in his life and thought. Their exact setting, in the process of his life, the progress of his philosophy, and the development of his poetic technique, will help to deepen and clarify the immediate, superficial recognition of their quality felt by every reader.

To begin with – and always regarding *To Autumn* as an off-shoot, a string retouched sympathetically by the earlier odes – these poems, together with the rejected *On Indolence*, were probably written in a much shorter space of time than is usually reckoned. Critics and biographers have seldom done full justice to the tremendous speed and concentration with which Keats worked. Looking, as one does here, at his often much-corrected manuscript, it is natural to assume that these corrections show a process of putting-aside and fresh consideration, lasting perhaps over days and weeks. This would have been quite foreign to Keats's outlook. 'My judgment', he himself explained, 'is as active while I am actually writing as my imagination. In fact all my faculties are strongly excited, & in their full play.' In other words, his own self-criticism enabled him to correct as he went along. He repudiated for himself the idea of later revision. 'And shall I afterwards,' he asked, 'when my imagination is idle, & the heat in which I wrote, has gone off, sit down coldly to criticise.'

We can say almost precisely, then, that Keats wrote his summer odes between 26 April and 18 May 1819; probably they were completed well before the latter date. The dates represent a period of exceptionally fine weather, and Keats was quite open about the effect the weather had on his inspiration. 'Give me fine weather', he exclaimed; and with special reference to just this patch of writing, he had remarked sadly in the middle of February 'to tell the truth I have not been in great cue for writing lately – I must wait for the spring to rouse me up a little'. This mood had continued for another six weeks, during which Keats wrote, again in his own words, 'nothing – nothing – nothing'; but when the spring did come, it emerged in a form that had all the rousing effect Keats could have wished. The first fortnight of April was delightful, so that, as he said, 'the lambs tails give a frisk extraordinary'. This friskiness communicated itself to his moribund muse, and the first half of the month was full of light verse, parodies and skits, all writing himself back into poetic form. By the beginning of the third week of April, this matured into haunting poetry, with the 'Dante' sonnet (16 April) and *La Belle Dame Sans Merci* on 21 April. The stage was set for some serious conscious effort; and the perfect morning of 26 April probably saw it begun. By 30 April, the *Ode to Psyche*, a poem instinct with all the loveliness of an enclosed summer garden, was completed. A creation of 'the gardener fancy' in the poem, it is at the same time a picture of the exact season 'in', as Keats wrote, 'delightful forwardness; the violets are not withered, before the peeping of the first rose'. All the other odes take up this theme of seasonal ease and delight, even *Indolence*, which seems to describe the one solitary, showery day on 4 May.

With Keats, it is not trivial to associate this simple climatic background with the fulfilment of the Odes; he was, as he wrote elsewhere, accustomed to regard nature 'for poetical purposes'. The place where this natural beauty was enjoyed is equally important. In 1815, two friends and namesakes, Charles Brown and Charles Wentworth Dilke, had begun to build a pair of semi-detached houses on Albion Grove at the bottom of Downshire Hill, Hampstead. By summer 1817, Keats had become acquainted with both, and was continually in and out of

8

this building, known, after Dilke's middle name, as Wentworth Place. In December 1818, with one brother abroad and one just dead, Keats came to live in the bachelor Brown's half of the establishment, sharing a common garden with Mr and Mrs Dilke and their small son, yet another Charles. A laurustinus hedge separated this from the still-open portion of Hampstead Heath. Within this boundary, the methodical and efficient Dilke had already established a well-ordered garden, with fruit-trees, shrubs and roses, shading and secluding the 'grass plot' or shared lawn. Although this part of Hampstead was just beginning to be suburbanized, and other houses were starting to be built, this garden was a domesticated outpost of the Heath, whose wild-life wandered in it; Dilke, typically practical, kept a gun for visiting birds and rabbits. Keats, in the few steps from breakfast room to grass plot, could sit under the plum-tree and withdraw into a green world, an Eden of fruit and flowers and animals; and, by now, the garden contained an Eve.

On 3 April 1819, after an agreeable masculine evening of claret-drinking, Dilke packed up his family and moved to Westminster. This decision, after all the care he had spent on the Hampstead house, was entirely due to another obsession of his over-conscientious mind, his only child's education. He wanted his boy to go to Westminster School; so he transplanted his kindly, easy-going wife and let his portion of Wentworth Place. The new tenants were already known to Keats. They had even occupied Brown's portion of the property when Keats and Brown were out of Hampstead the previous summer. Now they were neighbours, and it was a revolution in Keats's life. The autumn before, when he was nursing his dying brother Tom higher up the hill in Well Walk, Keats had met these people, Mrs Samuel Brawne, a widow, and her three children. By the eldest, Fanny, a girl of eighteen, he had been at once attracted. The opening stages of this attraction were chequered by circumstances, which set a stamp of difficulty on the affair that it never totally outwore. Keats's brother was dying, slowly and distressingly. Keats himself experienced the attractions of two other quite different women. One of them, his friend J. H. Reynolds's cousin, Jane Cox, was hardly older than Fanny, but far more experienced and sophisticated; the other, Isabella Jones, carried experience and sophistication to a degree that at first puzzled and perhaps finally alienated Keats, though he continued to visit her well-appointed rooms in a fashionable quarter of Bloomsbury. Fanny Brawne had also at times alienated him by an immature asperity and a manner that seemed to imitate even ridiculously the sophistications of

9

fashion that he had accepted in the others; but by the time of her arrival to be his neighbour, she had conquered his misgivings, and some sort of understanding, though not yet an official engagement, had grown between them. The assurance given by her close presence must be recognized as a moving spirit in these summer odes.

Such was the immediate physical and personal setting, to which must be added the heavy-handed but kindly supporting personality of Charles Brown, with his well-subscribed cellar, to which Keats contributed handsomely, and his hearty household, which even included a well-built female housekeeper who later became, in Regency style, Brown's mistress. Yet the profound moral and philosophical questionings of the Odes, which continue beneath Keats's thought all summer to their partial resolution in *To Autumn*, spring from a deep-laid train of experiences and conflicts that went back to the roots of his nature. The eldest boy of an orphaned family, Keats had early established a relationship with his two brothers 'passing the Love of Women'. He confessed this when one of them emigrated to America the previous summer; when in the winter the other died, Keats was left facing an overwhelming sensation of deprivation and misery to which he must adapt his whole being. His thought, always intensely active and realistic, had been for some time prepared for just this situation; but Keats himself knew and had expressed clearly the difference between an experience merely envisaged by philosophy and one 'proved', as he said, 'upon our pulses'. For several months, death and isolation had been presented to him in actual terms, which invaded his poetry. Keats's view of life had always been bound up with a full realization of death, 'from the early loss of our parents and even for earlier Misfortunes', as he himself put it; yet this attitude had not always been reflected in his poetry. From the death of Tom Keats, a human reality is added to what in his earlier poems had often been only an idea. Keats could have said with Wordsworth, also moved to great verse by the death of a brother, 'A deep distress hath humanised my Soul.' His poems from this time not only acquire a human urgency; the fact that life is shadowed by death never leaves them. The love-story of *The Eve of St Agnes* is played against a background of death and destruction, while some imminent doom hangs over the unfinished *Eve of St Mark*. The third and also unfinished book of *Hyperion* presents Apollo assuming his godhead through agonies that are only one degree this side of death. The occasional sonnets, and, most of all, *La Belle Dame Sans Merci*, the last great poem to be written before the Odes, make it clear

10

that all human experiences, love, poetry, the idealization of beauty must take place in the full knowledge of death and the total impermanence of earthly affairs. This is the keynote of all Keats's serious poems leading to the Odes, a returning theme through all the first few months of this year.

Further, however much Keats might stress the ideal of an unpremeditated type of poem, poetry for him was always conceived in what he called 'continual burning of thought'. His friend Dilke, commenting on this expression, added, 'Thought was intense with him, and seemed at times to assume a reality that influenced his conduct.' It clearly influenced his poetry; to find the origins of any burst of poetic writing by Keats, it is usually necessary to go back a month or two in his letters and see the thought and the philosophy expressed there, allowing an intervening few days or weeks for it to crystallize into verse. This is dramatically illustrated by the summer odes. For nearly three months, from 14 February to 3 May 1819, Keats was compiling an enormous journal letter for his brother George in America. It was a detailed record not only of his life, but of his thought, set out with every effort at true introspection. 'Do you not think I strive – to know myself?', he exclaimed to his brother. The origins of much in Keats's odes are found in two long passages of writing, one on 19 March and the other, nearer the Odes themselves, on 21 April. The first begins with phrases that are reproduced almost word-for-word in the rejected *Indolence* ode, and continues in terms that are echoed in all the published odes, the *Ode on Melancholy* in particular.

> This is the world – thus we cannot expect to give way many hours to pleasure – Circumstances are like Clouds continually gathering and bursting – While we are laughing the seed of some trouble is put into the wide arable land of events – while we are laughing it sprouts is (*for* it) grows and suddenly bears a poison fruit which we must pluck –

How should man deal with these casual disasters? Keats, later in the same passage, wrote it down as his faith that 'there is an ellectric fire in human nature tending to purify ... there is continually some birth of new heroism' to meet these events. The instinctive attitudes we fall into, so as to combat these attacks of chance, may be as pleasing to some 'superior being' as the instinctive, spontaneous actions and movements of the lesser animals may be to us.

This was as far as Keats had got by the middle of March. By 21 April, still beating at this question of the world as the place of 'an eternal fierce destruction', he had evolved tentatively for himself some sort of philosophic answer. More confidently, he put forward his suggestions to his brother as 'a grander system of salvation' than the Christian religion seemed to him able to provide. He still accepted the total impermanence of earthly things, in words that once more foreshadow the imagery of the Odes.

> For instance suppose a rose to have sensation, it blooms on a beautiful morning it enjoys itself – but there comes a cold wind, a hot sun – it cannot escape it, it cannot destroy its annoyances – they are as native to the world as itself – no more can man be happy ...

Keats, however, has now arrived at a stage in advance of his position a month before. He now does not desire nor even believe in the idea that the world should be perfect. A perfect life, lived under the overhanging knowledge of coming death, would be intolerable. The human being under this burden 'would leave this world as Eve left Paradise'. The troubles and pains of life must be with us for a good reason. What is the reason?

Keats at once rejected what he believed to be the Christian answer, that this world is anyway 'a vale of tears', from which we are to be redeemed to a rewarding, heavenly state. In doing so, he was obviously put off by the unctuous, evangelical phraseology of his time, which may have oppressed him specially on the occasion of his brother's funeral. His view, however, was more than an irritation at conventional clerical phrases. He did not believe that we are created with an individual soul, to be redeemed from the sin of this world by the intervention of a divine mediator. Rather he set out a system of explanation which he called 'Soul-making'. Assuming that we start with what he called an intelligence, defined as 'a spark of the divinity' and, even more boldly, 'sparks which are God', how are these to be made individual souls, each with a separate identity? Keats's answer was what he himself called a system of Spirit-creation. It was in elucidating this that he thought he had found, as much for his own comfort as anything else, a reason for the 'World of pains and troubles', of which he had had so recently such tragic and personal experience. If the soul, in whose immortality he still strongly believed, was not present at birth, but was to be individually formed by the time of death, what was the forming agency? Keats proposed that it should be just that array of difficult, testing and apparently arbitrary circumstances, 'like Clouds continually gathering and bursting', whose presence had so far oppressed his thought. These were the necessary methods by which the soul was to be made. 'Do you not see,' he cried, 'how necessary a

12

World of Pains and troubles is to school an Intelligence and make it a soul? A Place where the heart must feel and suffer in a thousand diverse ways!' The outwardly unreasonable and even cruel nature of the world might then be, as he had tried to persuade himself a month earlier, part of a divine plan, in order to create and perfect the soul during the passage of life on earth.

Keats was not so far off the Christian view in this as he supposed. Much of his argument, even down to particular images, resembles the case for Christianity itself put by Bishop Butler in his *The Analogy of Religion*. Keats had discussed this with theological friends, and was possibly even reading Butler at this time. The essential difference was that Butler, while stressing that the soul was improvable during life by just such a set of trials and provings that Keats postulated, believed the soul itself to be already created and present from birth; he also emphasized that, whatever the improvements wrought by the testings of Keats's 'world of Circumstances', the soul still remained imperfect enough to require the intervention and mediation of Christ, a notion which Keats would never accept. Nor is it quite certain how much, in the Odes, Keats accepted his own self-created philosophy of Soul-making. The poems all start with the same questions that had prompted this search for a satisfactory doctrine. They do not all come to such a complete answer. In the face of the manifest impermanence of life, much of the agonized questioning remains. The Odes all seek for evidence of a permanence which they cannot always reach. The beauty of Nature, typified by the song of the nightingale, may seem immortal; but is it truly? The poem ends with a question. 'Fled is that music: – Do I wake or sleep?' The immortality of Art, promised by the Grecian Urn, may be itself only the coldness of another kind of death. The acceptance of the world's transitoriness, counselled in the *Ode on Melancholy*, has some, but by no means all, of the positive hope of the doctrine of Soul-making. The soul may end only as a lifeless trophy of the world's battlefield. In the *Ode to Psyche*, the divinity of the soul, or psyche, is celebrated; the human trials and pains of Psyche are left unrecorded. Only in *To Autumn*, written later in the year, Keats seems to realize in poetry the full implication of his philosophy. By accepting the signs of decay and disappearance in all its surrounding world, the soul matures itself to a final completion.

Yet although the Odes may not fulfil themselves as an expression of the philosophy from which they arise, they are fulfilled technically as poems, and give, purely as art, a sense of completeness found hardly anywhere else in Keats's work. Together with a revaluation of his thought in this spring of 1819, he was attempting, perhaps more successfully, some reconstitution of his poetry; the Odes are the triumphant example of these new values. They are the final point in a life-long struggle in Keats's poetic life, if one can apply the term to a poetic output that had only started five years earlier, and was already in the middle of its last year. Much of Keats's writing life was haunted and often distracted by the belief that a great poem must be a long poem. He had precedents for this both in his wide reading of the Elizabethans and in many of the popular successes of his own time, but it was a belief that dangerously stretched his own immature powers, and laid him open to criticism that was not always unjust. His 'own domestic criticism', sharper even than the reviews, had pointed out to him that winter the 'slipshod' quality of much of his 4,000 line epic *Endymion*. On the night of 19 April, he had handed to his publishers his unfinished blank-verse epic, *Hyperion*, remarking that he was dissatisfied with what he had done of it, and that he would not complete it. Apart from other considerations, the scale alone seems to have daunted him. On the other hand, he was beginning to feel an equal dissatisfaction with a verse-form at the other end of the scale, the sonnet. Keats had written notably in both of the main types of sonnet, the so-called Petrarchan and Shakespearian; but his serious thought of the past few months now seemed to require a medium which, though formal, should not be too constrained. In his letter to George Keats, he pointed out the cramping effect of both kinds of sonnet. The rhymes in the Petrarchan, which only uses two rhymes in the first eight lines, had a 'pouncing' or automatic effect. The Shakespearian, with three quatrains and end couplet, was what he called 'too elegaic' or slack, and the final couplet was awkward. Just as he had evolved the idea of Soul-making to avoid the constrictions of Christian doctrine, so he wished for a sonnet-form that would carry these larger thoughts. He copied three experimental sonnets for George, but even their variants did not please him. Something compact and yet more massive was needed.

His stepping-stone to this new form was the *Ode to Psyche*, also copied in this letter, with the remark that it was done 'leisurely' and with 'moderate pains', though, as we have seen, this may not indicate more than three or four days' work, probably from 26 to 30 April. This ode, the first-fruits of his need to give his thought-processes a more satisfying shape, is a hybrid. Keats was studying at the time the loose 'Pindaric' odes of Dryden; their diffuseness, and especially their

14

use of repetition, found their way into *Psyche*. Yet there is a stiffening in the way the long stanzas are handled that certainly comes from his experiments with the sonnet. Just a year earlier, Keats had written the one poem which he himself had, until this time, called an Ode. To be exact, he had written one stanza before the 'Circumstances' of life, with which his greater odes were to deal, had interrupted him. This one stanza of an *Ode to Maia* has, in fact, the fourteen lines of a sonnet, though greatly varied, rearranged, and, in some instances, shortened. His new interest in extending the sonnet revived some of the methods of this early experiment; sonnet-patterns, very like those used in the *Ode to Maia*, can be traced throughout the *Ode to Psyche*, and these are what give it the underlying unity without constraint at which Keats was aiming. One final attempt to vary the sonnet – in a sonnet on the Sonnet itself – then led him to the form which he was to adopt, with only trifling exceptions, for all the subsequent odes.

The stanza he now shaped is so simple, and so easily derived from the two kinds of sonnet, that it has sometimes been doubted whether his mind really worked in this way; but the evidence of his own letter, and the fact that he retained its effect basically for all the great odes, including the lesser *Indolence*, seem to show that the needs of both philosophy and poetry had met in this direct and simple course. Roughly, Keats took one quatrain of the Shakespearian-type sonnet, and added to it the sestet of a Petrarchan. The ten-line stanza thus produced could be repeated several times – though never, in practice, more than eight – to produce a poem of substance and yet of unity. The variations on this elementary plan are, of course, many and subtle, but the broad outline in all the summer odes is the same, and strengthens the sensation that they were written within a few days of one another. They form, it might be said, an ode-sequence, with more force and authority than could have been given by a sonnet-sequence on the same themes. When Keats came to write *To Autumn*, he seems to have wished to give an even greater authority, a sense of solidity and judgement to the stanzas of a poem which, unlike the other odes, is a work of statement rather than of questioning. Probably at first unconsciously, though then with deliberate intent, he added an extra line to the sestet, which became a septet, and created a stanza of eleven lines. The clinching weight of the conclusion of this poem is largely due to this simple variation on the scheme used for the earlier summer odes.

Both in technique and in philosophy, then, the Odes of the 1820 volume are an expression of Keats's thought in April 1819. It was a time when his mind and his creative impulses were working at their keenest; when the fullest apprehension of the world around him and the unseen world of ideas had not been dulled or deflected by the coming symptoms of the fatal illness that carried him off within the next two years. His nature, always striving for a Shakespearian universality, seemed miraculously to have achieved this aim, and to have shaken itself free from the ultimately insuperable difficulties that crushed, though they did not finally conquer it. It is this universal quality in the Odes, the sense of pure creation, that conveys itself most strongly to the reader. They are the signature and handwriting of a great spirit; and as we watch his hand physically trace them, we share to some degree in that spiritual triumph.

THE TEXTS IN THE 1820 EDITION

reprinted by permission of the Clarendon Press,
Oxford

ODE TO A NIGHTINGALE

My heart aches, and a drowsy numbness pains
   My sense, as though of hemlock I had drunk,
Or emptied some dull opiate to the drains
   One minute past, and Lethe-wards had sunk:
'Tis not through envy of thy happy lot,
   But being too happy in thine happiness,—
      That thou, light-winged Dryad of the trees,
        In some melodious plot
Of beechen green, and shadows numberless,
   Singest of summer in full-throated ease.

O, for a draught of vintage! that hath been
   Cool'd a long age in the deep-delved earth,
Tasting of Flora and the country green,
   Dance, and Provençal song, and sunburnt mirth!
O for a beaker full of the warm South,
   Full of the true, the blushful Hippocrene,
      With beaded bubbles winking at the brim,
        And purple-stained mouth;
That I might drink, and leave the world unseen,
   And with thee fade away into the forest dim:

Fade far away, dissolve, and quite forget
   What thou among the leaves hast never known,
The weariness, the fever, and the fret
   Here, where men sit and hear each other groan;
Where palsy shakes a few, sad, last gray hairs,
   Where youth grows pale, and spectre-thin, and dies;
      Where but to think is to be full of sorrow
         And leaden-eyed despairs,
Where Beauty cannot keep her lustrous eyes,
   Or new Love pine at them beyond to-morrow.

Away! away! for I will fly to thee,
   Not charioted by Bacchus and his pards,
But on the viewless wings of Poesy,
   Though the dull brain perplexes and retards:
Already with thee! tender is the night,
   And haply the Queen-Moon is on her throne,
      Cluster'd around by all her starry Fays;
         But here there is no light,
Save what from heaven is with the breezes blown
      Through verdurous glooms and winding mossy
         ways.

I cannot see what flowers are at my feet,
    Nor what soft incense hangs upon the boughs,
But, in embalmed darkness, guess each sweet
    Wherewith the seasonable month endows
The grass, the thicket, and the fruit-tree wild;
    White hawthorn, and the pastoral eglantine;
        Fast fading violets cover'd up in leaves;
            And mid-May's eldest child,
The coming musk-rose, full of dewy wine,
    The murmurous haunt of flies on summer eves.

Darkling I listen; and, for many a time
    I have been half in love with easeful Death,
Call'd him soft names in many a mused rhyme,
    To take into the air my quiet breath;
Now more than ever seems it rich to die,
    To cease upon the midnight with no pain,
        While thou art pouring forth thy soul abroad
            In such an ecstasy!
Still wouldst thou sing, and I have ears in vain—
    To thy high requiem become a sod.

Thou wast not born for death, immortal Bird!
No hungry generations tread thee down;
The voice I hear this passing night was heard
In ancient days by emperor and clown:
Perhaps the self-same song that found a path
Through the sad heart of Ruth, when, sick for home,
She stood in tears amid the alien corn;
The same that oft-times hath
Charm'd magic casements, opening on the foam
Of perilous seas, in faery lands forlorn.

Forlorn! the very word is like a bell
To toll me back from thee to my sole self!
Adieu! the fancy cannot cheat so well
As she is fam'd to do, deceiving elf.
Adieu! adieu! thy plaintive anthem fades
Past the near meadows, over the still stream,
Up the hill-side; and now 'tis buried deep
In the next valley-glades:
Was it a vision, or a waking dream?
Fled is that music:—Do I wake or sleep?

ODE ON A GRECIAN URN

Thou still unravish'd bride of quietness,
　　Thou foster-child of silence and slow time,
Sylvan historian, who canst thus express
　　A flowery tale more sweetly than our rhyme:
What leaf-fring'd legend haunts about thy shape
　　Of deities or mortals, or of both,
　　　　In Tempe or the dales of Arcady?
　　What men or gods are these? What maidens loth?
What mad pursuit? What struggle to escape?
　　　　What pipes and timbrels? What wild ecstasy?

Heard melodies are sweet, but those unheard
　　Are sweeter; therefore, ye soft pipes, play on;
Not to the sensual ear, but, more endear'd,
　　Pipe to the spirit ditties of no tone:
Fair youth, beneath the trees, thou canst not leave
　　Thy song, nor ever can those trees be bare;
　　　　Bold Lover, never, never canst thous kiss,
Though winning near the goal—yet, do not grieve;
　　She cannot fade, though thou hast not thy bliss,
　　　　For ever wilt thou love, and she be fair!

Ah, happy, happy boughs! that cannot shed
  Your leaves, nor ever bid the Spring adieu;
And, happy melodist, unwearied,
  For ever piping songs for ever new;
More happy love! more happy, happy love!
  For ever warm and still to be enjoy'd,
    For ever panting, and for ever young;
All breathing human passion far above,
  That leaves a heart high-sorrowful and cloy'd,
    A burning forehead, and a parching tongue.

Who are these coming to the sacrifice?
  To what green altar, O mysterious priest,
Lead'st thou that heifer lowing at the skies,
  And all her silken flanks with garlands drest?
What little town by river or sea shore,
  Or mountain-built with peaceful citadel,
    Is emptied of this folk, this pious morn?
And, little town, thy streets for evermore
  Will silent be; and not a soul to tell
    Why thou art desolate, can e'er return.

O Attic shape! Fair attitude! with brede
　　Of marble men and maidens overwrought,
With forest branches and the trodden weed;
　　Thou, silent form, dost tease us out of thought
As doth eternity: Cold Pastoral!
　　When old age shall this generation waste,
　　　　Thou shalt remain, in midst of other woe
Than ours, a friend to man, to whom thou say'st,
　　"Beauty is truth, truth beauty,"—that is all
　　　　Ye know on earth, and all ye need to know.

ODE TO PSYCHE

O Goddess ! hear these tuneless numbers, wrung
 By sweet enforcement and remembrance dear,
And pardon that thy secrets should be sung
 Even into thine own soft-conched ear :
Surely I dreamt to-day, or did I see
 The winged Psyche with awaken'd eyes ?
I wander'd in a forest thoughtlessly,
 And, on the sudden, fainting with surprise,
Saw two fair creatures, couched side by side
 In deepest grass, beneath the whisp'ring roof
 Of leaves and trembled blossoms, where there ran
  A brooklet, scarce espied :
'Mid hush'd, cool-rooted flowers, fragrant-eyed,
 Blue, silver-white, and budded Tyrian,
They lay calm-breathing on the bedded grass ;
 Their arms embraced, and their pinions too ;
 Their lips touch'd not, but had not bade adieu,
As if disjoined by soft-handed slumber,
And ready still past kisses to outnumber
 At tender eye-dawn of aurorean love :
  The winged boy I knew ;
 But who wast thou, O happy, happy dove ?
  His Psyche true !

O latest born and loveliest vision far
  Of all Olympus' faded hierarchy !
Fairer than Phœbe's sapphire-region'd star,
  Or Vesper, amorous glow-worm of the sky ;
Fairer than these, though temple thou hast none,
    Nor altar heap'd with flowers ;
Nor virgin-choir to make delicious moan
    Upon the midnight hours ;
No voice, no lute, no pipe, no incense sweet
  From chain-swung censer teeming ;
No shrine, no grove, no oracle, no heat
  Of pale-mouth'd prophet dreaming.

O brightest ! though too late for antique vows,
  Too, too late for the fond believing lyre,
When holy were the haunted forest boughs,
  Holy the air, the water, and the fire ;
Yet even in these days so far retir'd
  From happy pieties, thy lucent fans,
  Fluttering among the faint Olympians,
I see, and sing, by my own eyes inspired.
So let me be thy choir, and make a moan
    Upon the midnight hours ;
Thy voice, thy lute, thy pipe, thy incense sweet
  From swinged censer teeming ;
Thy shrine, thy grove, thy oracle, thy heat
  Of pale-mouth'd prophet dreaming.

Yes, I will be thy priest, and build a fane
    In some untrodden region of my mind,
Where branched thoughts, new grown with pleasant
        pain,
    Instead of pines shall murmur in the wind:
Far, far around shall those dark-cluster'd trees
    Fledge the wild-ridged mountains steep by steep;
And there by zephyrs, streams, and birds, and bees,
    The moss-lain Dryads shall be lull'd to sleep;
And in the midst of this wide quietness
A rosy sanctuary will I dress
With the wreath'd trellis of a working brain,
    With buds, and bells, and stars without a name,
With all the gardener Fancy e'er could feign,
    Who breeding flowers, will never breed the same:
And there shall be for thee all soft delight
    That shadowy thought can win,
A bright torch, and a casement ope at night,
    To let the warm Love in!

TO AUTUMN

Season of mists and mellow fruitfulness,
　　Close bosom-friend of the maturing sun;
Conspiring with him how to load and bless
　　With fruit the vines that round the thatch-eves run;
To bend with apples the moss'd cottage-trees,
　　And fill all fruit with ripeness to the core;
　　　To swell the gourd, and plump the hazel shells
With a sweet kernel; to set budding more,
　　And still more, later flowers for the bees,
　　Until they think warm days will never cease,
　　　For Summer has o'er-brimm'd their clammy cells.

Who hath not seen thee oft amid thy store?
　　Sometimes whoever seeks abroad may find
Thee sitting careless on a granary floor,
　　Thy hair soft-lifted by the winnowing wind;
Or on a half-reap'd furrow sound asleep,
　　Drows'd with the fume of poppies, while thy hook
　　　Spares the next swath and all its twined flowers:
And sometimes like a gleaner thou dost keep
　　Steady thy laden head across a brook;
　　Or by a cyder-press, with patient look,
　　　Thou watchest the last oozings hours by hours.

Where are the songs of Spring ? Ay, where are they ?
  Think not of them, thou hast thy music too,—
While barred clouds bloom the soft-dying day,
  And touch the stubble-plains with rosy hue ;
Then in a wailful choir the small gnats mourn
  Among the river sallows, borne aloft
    Or sinking as the light wind lives or dies ;
And full-grown lambs loud bleat from hilly bourn ;
  Hedge-crickets sing ; and now with treble soft
  The red-breast whistles from a garden-croft ;
    And gathering swallows twitter in the skies.

ODE ON MELANCHOLY

No, no, go not to Lethe, neither twist
    Wolf's-bane, tight-rooted, for its poisonous wine;
Nor suffer thy pale forehead to be kiss'd
    By nightshade, ruby grape of Proserpine;
Make not your rosary of yew-berries,
    Nor let the beetle, nor the death-moth be
      Your mournful Psyche, nor the downy owl
A partner in your sorrow's mysteries;
    For shade to shade will come too drowsily,
      And drown the wakeful anguish of the soul.

But when the melancholy fit shall fall
    Sudden from heaven like a weeping cloud,
That fosters the droop-headed flowers all,
    And hides the green hill in an April shroud;
Then glut thy sorrow on a morning rose,
    Or on the rainbow of the salt sand-wave,
      Or on the wealth of globed peonies;
Or if thy mistress some rich anger shows,
    Emprison her soft hand, and let her rave,
      And feed deep, deep upon her peerless eyes.

She dwells with Beauty—Beauty that must die ;
   And Joy, whose hand is ever at his lips
Bidding adieu ; and aching Pleasure nigh,
    Turning to poison while the bee-mouth sips :
Ay, in the very temple of Delight
    Veil'd Melancholy has her sovran shrine,
      Though seen of none save him whose strenuous
          tongue
Can burst Joy's grape against his palate fine ;
    His soul shall taste the sadness of her might,
      And be among her cloudy trophies hung.

THE EARLIEST KNOWN MANUSCRIPTS

Location and sizes of the manuscripts

ODE TO A NIGHTINGALE

Fitzwilliam Museum, Cambridge. Written in ink on paper, watermarked RUSE & TURNERS 1817. Each half sheet measures 20·5 cm. ×12 cm. Reproduced by permission of the Syndics of the Fitzwilliam Museum.

ODE ON A GRECIAN URN

(In the hand of George Keats.) British Museum, Egerton MS. 2780, ff. 55–56. Page size 7 in.×$4\frac{3}{8}$ in.

ODE TO PSYCHE

Pierpont Morgan Library, New York. Written on a single sheet of white wove paper, folded to form four pages measuring $8\frac{11}{16}$ in.×$7\frac{1}{4}$ in. The half forming pp. 3 and 4 is embossed at the inside bottom with 'BATH' surmounted by a crown, the entire blind stamp being upside down. Written in brown ink on pp. 1, 2 and 3, with p. 4 blank. The manuscript is bound in a volume of green crushed morocco, red silk doublures, by Bradstreet, and is accompanied in that volume by a letter from Keats to John Taylor of Taylor and Hessey, Publishers, dated by postmark 17 November 1819.

TO AUTUMN

Houghton Library, Harvard University, Cambridge, Mass. Page size $10\frac{13}{16}$ in.×$7\frac{3}{4}$ in.

ODE ON MELANCHOLY

First two stanzas: Robert H. Taylor, Princeton, New Jersey. Wove paper, page size 7 in.×$4\frac{1}{4}$ in.

Last stanza: Henry W. and Albert A. Berg Collection of The New York Public Library, Astor, Lenox and Tilden Foundations, page size $7\frac{1}{4}$ in.×$4\frac{7}{16}$ in.

N.B. *Where Keats has written words or letters directly on top of others, the original word is printed in the text and the altered word marked with an asterisk at the foot of the page*

drowsy
~~My~~ Heart aches and a ~~painful~~ numbness ~~falls~~.
                                              pains
My sense as though of hemlock I had drunk
Or emptid some dull opiate to the drains
                  past
One minute ~~hence~~, and Lethe-wards had sunk.
'Tis not through envy of thy happy lot,
But being too happy in thine happiness,
That thou light-winged dryad of the trees
In some melodious plot
Of beechen green, and shadows numberless
Singest of summer in full-throated ease.
O for a draught of vintage that has been
            long
Cooling an age in the deep-delved earth
Tasting of Flora, and the country green
~~And~~ Dance, and povencal song and sunburnt mirth
O for a Beaker full of the warm South,
Full of the true and blushful Hippocrene
With cluster'd bubbles winking at the brim
And puple stained mouth,
That I might drink and leave the world unseen
And with thee fade away into the forest dim
Fade far away, dissolve and quite forget
What thou among the leaves hast never known
The weariness, the feavr and the fret
Here, where Men sit and hear each other groan
Where palsy shakes a few sad last grey hairs
                    spectre
Where youth grows pale and thin, ~~and old~~
                                    and dies

*Cooled

Ode to the Nightingale

My Heart aches and a ~~painful~~ drowsy numbness ~~falls~~

My sense, as though of hemlock I had drunk

Or emptied some dull opiate to the drains

One minute ~~since~~ past, and Lethe-wards had sunk.

Tis not through envy of thy happy lot

But being too happy in thine happiness

~~That~~ thou light-winged dryad of the trees

In some melodious plot

Of beechen green, and shadows numberless

Singest of summer in full-throated ease.

O for a draught of vintage that has been

Cooling an long age in the deep-delved earth

Tasting of Flora, and the country green

~~And~~ Dance, and provencal song and sunburnt mirth

O for a Beaker full of the warm South,

Full of the true and blushful Hippocrene

With clustered bubbles winking at the brim

And purple stained mouth

That I might drink and ~~leave~~ the world unseen

And with thee fade away into ~~the~~ forest dim —

Fade far away, dissolve and quite forget

What thou among the leaves hast never known

The weariness, the fever and the fret

Here, where Men sit and hear each other groan

Where palsy shakes a few sad last grey hairs

Where ~~~~ grows pale and thin ~~~~ and dies

Where but to think is to be full of ~~grief~~

And leaden eyed despairs —

Where Beauty cannot keep her lustrous eyes

new

Or ^Love pine at them beyond tomorrow —

to

Away — away — for I will fly ~~with~~ thee

and

Not charioted by Bacchus ~~and~~ his Pards

But on the viewless wings of Poesy,

Though the dull brain perplexes and retards —

Already with thee! tender is the night

And haply the Queen-moon is on her throne

~~Clusted~~ around by all her starry fays —

But here there is no light

heaven

Save what from is with the breezes brown

~~Sidelong~~ Though veduous glooms and winding mossy

ways —

I cannot see what flowers are at my feet

Nor what ~~blooms~~ soft insence hangs upon the

boughs

But in embalmed darkness guess each sweet

~~With with~~

Wherewith the seasonable month endows

The grass the thicket and the fruit tree wild

White Hawthorn and the pastoral eglantine

Fast fading violets covered up in leaves

And midmay's eldest child

The coming muskrose full of sweetest wine

* Her murmurous hant of flies on summer eves

Small, winged Dryad

*The

38

Where but to think is to be full of ~~and~~ sorrow

And leaden eyed despairs

Where Beauty cannot keep her lustrous eye

Or new Love pine at them beyond tomorrow—

Away—Away—for I will fly to thee ~~with~~

Not charioted by Bacchus ~~and~~ and his Pards

But on the viewless wings of Poesy

Though the dull brain perplexes and retards—

Already with thee! tender is the night

And haply the Queen moon is on her throne

~~Clusted~~ around by all her starry Fays—

But here there is no light

Save what from heaven is with the breezes blown

~~Through~~ Through verdurous glooms and winding mossy ways—

I cannot see what flowers are at my feet

Nor what ~~blooms~~ soft incense hangs upon the

But in embalmed darkness guess each sweet boughs

~~With~~ Wherewith the seasonable month endows

The grass the Thicket and the fruit tree wild

White Hawthorn and the pastoral eglantine

Fast fading violets covered up in leaves

And mid may's eldest child

The coming musk rose full of nectar wine

The murmurous haunt of flies on summer eves

Darkling I listen, and for many a time
        been
  I have half in love with easeful death
Call'd him soft names in many a mused rhyme,
   To take into the air my painless breath
 Now, more than ever seems it rich to die
 To cease upon the midnight with no pain
 While though art pouring thus thy soul abroad
  In such an Extacy —
 Still would thou sing and I have years in vain
 But requiem'd

      o
   For thy high requiem, become a sod —

Thou wast not born for death, immortal Bird
    No hungry generations tread thee down,
The voice I hear this passing night was heard
   In ancient days by Emperour and Clown
         song
 Perhaps the selfsame voice that found a path
 Though the sad heart of Ruth, when sick for home
 She stood in tears amid the alien corn.
 The same that oftimes hath
       magic
 Cham'd the wide casements opening on the foam
 Of kuthless perilous seas in fairy lands folorn

Darkling I listen; and, for many a time
I have been half in love with easeful death
Call'd him soft names in many a mused rhyme,
To take into the air my painless breath
Now more than ever seems it rich to die.
To cease upon the midnight with no pain
While thou art pouring thus thy soul abroad
In such an Ecstacy —
Still would thou sing and I have ears in vain
But ~~in~~ ~~sounds~~
For thy high requiem, become a sod —

Thou wast not born for death, immortal Bird
No hungry generations tread thee down;
The voice I hear this passing night was heard
In ancient days by Emperour and Clown
                                    soul
Perhaps the selfsame ~~voice~~ that found a path
Through the sad heart of Ruth, when sick for home
She stood in tears amid the alien corn.
The same that oftimes hath
                   magic
Chann'd the ~~wide~~ casements opening on the foam
Of ~~perilous~~ perilous seas in fairy lands folorn.

I

Folorn! the very world is like a bell
                    me back
        To told ~~bae me~~ from thee unto myself
Adieu! the fancy cannot cheat so well
                                    ving
        As she is fam'd to do, decei~~tful~~ elf!
        Adieu! Adieu! thy plaintuve Anthem fades
        Past the near meadows, over the still stream,
        Up the hill side, and now 'tis buried deep
        In the next vally's glades —
        Was it a vision real or waking dream? —
        Fled is that Music — do I wake or sleep?

        *toll

*

Forlorn! the very word is like a bell
      To toll me back   from thee unto myself
Adieu! the fancy cannot cheat so well
      As she is fam'd to do, deceiving elf!
Adieu! Adieu! thy plaintive Anthem fades
Past the near meadows, over the still stream,
      Up the hill side, and now 'tis buried deep
In the next valley glades.
Was it a vision real or waking dream?
      Fled is that Music - do I wake or sleep?

1

Thou still unravish'd bride of quietness,
    Thou foster child of silence and slow time,
Sylvan Historian, who can'st thus express
    A flowery tale more sweetly than our rhyme, —
What leaf-fring'd legend haunts about thy shape,
    Of Deities, or mortals, or of both
        In Tempe, or the Dales of Arcady?
    What men or Gods are these? what maidens loth?
What love? what dance? what struggle to escape?
        What pipes and timbrels? what wild extacy?

2

Heard melodies are sweet, but those unheard
    Are sweeter, — therefore ye soft pipes play on;
Not to the sensual ear, but, more endear'd,
    Pipe to the spirit-ditties of no tone;
Fair Youth, beneath the trees thou can'st not leave
    Thy song, nor ever can those trees be bare, —
        Bold lover, never, never can'st thou kiss,
Tho' winning near the goal, — O, do not grieve!
    She cannot fade, tho' thou hast not thy bliss
        For ever wilt thou love, and she be fair!

Ode on a Grecian Urn 1819.

1

Thou still unravish'd bride of quietness,
 Thou foster child of silence and slow time,
Sylvan Historian, who can'st thus express
 A flowery tale more sweetly than our rhyme,—
What leaf-fring'd legend haunts about thy shape,
 Of Deities, or mortals, or of both
  In Tempe, or the Dales of Arcady?
 What men or Gods are these? what maidens loth?
What love? what dance? what struggle to escape?
 What pipes and timbrels? what wild extacy?

2

Heard melodies are sweet, but those unheard
 Are sweeter,—therefore ye soft pipes play on;
Not to the sensual ear, but, more endear'd,
 Pipe to the spirit-ditties of no tone;
Fair Youth, beneath the trees thou can'st not leave
 Thy song, nor ever can those trees be bare,—
  Bold lover, never, never can'st thou kiss.
Tho' winning near the goal,—O, do not grieve!
 She cannot fade, tho' thou hast not thy bliss
For ever wilt thou love, and she be fair!

3

Ah! happy, happy boughs! that cannot shed
    Your leaves, nor ever bid the spring adieu;
And happy melodist! unwearied
    For ever piping songs for ever new;
More happy love! more happy, happy love!
    For ever warm, and still to be enjoyed,
        For ever panting, and for ever young,
All breathing human Passion far above,
    That leaves a heart high sorrowful and cloy'd,
        A burning forehead and a parching tongue.

4

Who are these coming to the Sacrifice?
    To what green Altar, O mysterious Priest!
Lead'st thou that Heifer lowing at the skies,
    And all her silken sides with garlands drest?
What little town, by river or sea shore,
    Or mountain built with peaceful citadel,
        Is emptied of this folk, this pious morn?
And, little Town, thy streets, for evermore,
    Will silent be, and not a soul, to tell
        Why thou art desolate, can e'er return.

Ah! happy, happy boughs! that cannot shed
  Your leaves, nor ever bid the spring adieu;
And happy melodist! unwearied
  For ever piping songs for ever new;
More happy love! more happy, happy love!
  For ever warm, and still to be enjoyed,
    For ever panting, and for ever young,
All breathing human Passion far above,
  That leaves a heart high sorrowful and cloy'd,
    A burning forehead and a parching tongue.

4

Who are these coming to the Sacrifice?
  To what green Altar, O mysterious Priest!
Lead'st thou that Heifer lowing at the skies,
  And all her silken sides with garlands drest?
What little town, by river or sea shore,
  Or mountain built with peaceful citadel,
    Is emptied of this folk, this pious morn?
And, little Town, thy streets, for evermore
  Will silent be, and not a soul, to tell
    Why thou art desolate, can e'er return.

O Attic shape! fair attitude! with brede
    Of marble men and maidens, overwrought
        the
With forest-branches and trodden weed, —
    Thou silent form dost tease us out of thought
As doth Eternity! cold Pastoral,
    When old age shall this generation waste,
        Thou wilt remain in midst of other woe
Than our's, as friend to man, to whom thou say'st,
    Beauty is truth, — Truth Beauty, — that is all
        Ye know on Earth, and all ye need to know.

O Attic shape! fair attitude! with brede
Of marble men and maidens, overwrought
With forest-branches and the trodden weed,—
Thou silent form dost tease us out of thought
As doth Eternity! cold Pastoral,
When old-age shall this generation waste,
Thou wilt remain, in midst of other woe
Than our's, as friend to man, to whom thou say'st
Beauty is truth,—Truth Beauty,—that is all
Ye know on Earth, and all ye need to know.

ODE TO PSYCHE

O Goddess! hear these tuneless numbers, wrung
 By sweet enforcement, and remembrance dear,
And pardon that thy secrets should be sung
 Even into thine own soft-chonched ear!
Surely I drĕmt to day; or did I see,
 The winged Psyche, with awaken'd eyes?
I wander'd in a forest thoughtlessly,
 And on the sudden, fainting with surprise,
Saw two fair Creatures couched side by side,
In deepest grass, beneath the whispering fan
Of leaves and trembled blossoms, where there ran
A Brooklet scarce espied.
Mid
~~In~~ hush'd, cool-rooted flowers, fragrant eyed,
freckle pink Blue, silver-white, and budded syrian,
 They lay, calm-breathing, on the bedded grass,
Their arms embraced and their pinions too;
Their lips touch'd not, but had not bid adieu
As if disjoined by soft handed slumber,
And ready still past kisses to out number
At tender ~~dawning~~ eye-dawn of aurorian Love.
The winged Boy I knew:
But who wast thou O happy happy dove?
His Psyche true!

O latest born, and loveliest vision far
 Of all Olympus' faded Hierarchy!
      orb'd Phoebe's
Fairer than ~~Night's wide full~~, sapphire-region'd, star
 Or Vesper amorous glow worm of the sky;

Ode. To Psyche

O Goddess! hear these tuneless numbers, wrung
  By sweet enforcement and remembrance dear,
And pardon that thy secrets should be sung
  Even into thine own soft-conched ear!
Surely I dreamt to day; or did I see,
  The winged Psyche with awaken'd eyes?
I wander'd in a forest thoughtlessly,
  And on the sudden, fainting with surprize,
Saw two fair Creatures couched side by side,
  In deepest grass, beneath the whispering fan
Of leaves and trembled blossoms, where there ran
  A Brooklet scarce espied.

'Mid hush'd, cool-rooted flowers, fragrant eyed,
  Blue, silver-white, and budded syrian,
They lay, calm-breathing on the bedded grass.
  Their arms embraced and their pinions too;
  Their lips touch'd not but had not bid adieu,
As if disjoined by soft-handed slumber,
And ready still past Kisses to out number
  At tender ~~dawning~~ eye-dawn of aurorian Love.
  The winged Boy I knew:
But who wast thou O happy happy dove?
  His Psyche true!

O latest born, and loveliest vision far
  Of all Olympus' faded Hierarchy!
Fairer than ~~Phœbe's~~ ~~moonlight~~ sapphire-region'd star
  Or Vesper amorous glow worm of the sky;

Fairer than these though Temple thou hast none,
Nor Altar heap'd with flowers;
Nor Virgin Choir to make melodious moan
Upon the midnight hours;
Nor voice, nor lute, nor pipe, nor incense sweet
From chain-swung Censer teeming,
Nor Shrine, nor grove, nor Oracle, nor heat
Of pale-mouth'd Prophet dreaming.

O Bloomiest! though too late for antique vows
Too, too late for the fond believing Lyre,
When holy were the haunted forest-boughs,
Holy the Air, the Water, and the Fire:
Yet even in these days so far retir'd
From happy Pieties, thy lucent fans,
                    among
Fluttering ~~above~~ the faint Olympians,
                       own
I see, and sing by my ~~clear~~ eyes inspired.
O let me be thy Choir and make a moan
Upon the midnight hours;
Thy Voice, thy lute, thy Pipe, thy insence sweet
    From
~~Thy~~ swinged Censer teeming;
Thy Shrine, thy Grove, thy oracle, thy heat
Of Pale mouth'd Prophet dreaming!

Fairer than these though Temple thou hast none,
Nor Altar heap'd with flowers;
Nor Virgin Choir to make melodious moan
Upon the midnight hours;
Nor voice, nor lute, nor pipe, nor incense sweet
From chain-swang Censer teeming;
Nor Shrine, nor grove, nor Oracle, nor heat
Of pale-mouth'd Prophet dreaming.

O Bloomiest! though too late for antique vows
Too, too late for the fond believing lyre,
When holy were the haunted forest-boughs,
Holy the air, the Water, and the Fire:
Yet even in these days so far retir'd
From happy Pieties, thy lucent fans,
Fluttering among the faint Olympians,
I see, and sing by my own eyes inspired.
O let me be thy Choir and make a moan
Upon the midnight hours;
Thy Voice, thy lute, thy Pipe, thy incense sweet
From thy swinged Censer teeming;
Thy Shrine, thy Grove, thy oracle, thy heat
Of pale mouth'd Prophet dreaming!

Yes, I will be thy Priest and build a Fane
In some untrodden Region of my mind,
Where branched thoughts, new grown with pleasant pain
Instead of Pines shall murmur in the wind.
Far, far around shall those dark-cluster'd trees
Fledge the wild ridged mountains steep by steep;
And there by Zephyrs, streams, and birds and Bees
The moss-lain Dryads shall be lull'd to sleep.
And in the midst of this wide Quietness
A rosy sanctuary will I dress
With the wreath'd trellis of a working brain,
With buds and bells and stars without a name,
With all the gardener-Fancy e'er could feign,
breeding flowers will breed
Who plucking a thousand flower and never plucks the same
So bower'd Goddess will I worship thee
And there shall be for thee all soft delight
That shadowy thought can win
A bright torch, and a casement ope at night
the
To let warm Love glide in.

Yes. I will be thy Priest and build a Fane
In some untrodden Region of my mind,
Where branched thoughts, new grown with pleasant pain
Instead of Pines shall murmur in the wind.
Far, far around shall those dark-cluster'd trees
Fledge the-wild-ridged mountains steep by steep;
And there by Zephyrs, streams, and birds and Bees
The moss-lain Dryads shall be lull'd to sleep.
And in the midst of this wide Quietness
A rosy sanctuary, will I dress
With the wreath'd trellis of a working brain,
With buds and bells and stars without a name.—
With all the gardener-Fancy e'er could feign,
                                                bred
Who ~~plucking~~ breeding a ~~thousand flower~~ flowers and ~~never plucks~~ the same
~~So loues'd Goddess will I worship~~ ~~thee~~
And there shall be for thee all soft delight
That shadowy thought can win.
a bright torch, and a casement ope at night
              the
To let ~~warm~~ Love glide in.

Season of Mists and mellow fruitfulness
　　Close bosom friend of the maturing sun
　Conspiring with him how to load and bless
　　　The Vines with fruit that round the thatch eves run
　　　To bend with apples the moss'd cottage trees
　　　And fill all furuits with sweeness to the core
　　　　To swell the gourd, and plump the hazle shells
　　　　†sweet
　　With a white kernel; to set budding more
　　And still more later flowers for the bees
　　　Until they think wam days with never cease
　　　For Summer has o'erbrimm'd their clammy cells —

　　　　　　　　　　　oft amid thy stores?
Who hath not seen thee? ~~for thy haunts are many~~
　　　　　　　　　　　abroad
　　Sometimes whoeever seeks ~~for thee~~ may find
　Thee sitting careless on a granary floorr
　　Thy hair soft lifted by the winnowing wing　　　　*
　　　　　　　　　　　husky
　　　~~While bright the Sun slants through the barn~~; —
　　on on a half reap'd furrow sound asleep
　　~~Or sound asleep in a half reaped field~~

　　　Dosed with read poppies; while thy reeping hook

~~Spares form some slumbrous~~
　　　　　　　~~minutes while warm slumpers creep~~

　　Or on a half reap'd furrow sound asleep
　　　Dos'd with the fume of poppies, while thy hook
　　　Spares the next swath and all its twined flowers
　　　~~Spares for some slumbrous minutes the next swath;~~
　　　And sometimes like a gleaner thost dost keep
　　　Steady thy laden head across the brook;
　　　Or by a Cyder-press with patent look
　　　Thou watchest the last oozing hours by hours

　*wind

　†*Word faintly written, apparently by a later hand*

Season of Mists and mellow fruitfulness
  Close bosom friend of the maturing sun;
Conspiring with him how to load and bless
  The Vines with fruit that round the thatch eves run
    To bend with apples the mossd Cottage trees
    And fill all fruits with ripeness to the core
      To swell the gourd, and plump the hazle shells
With a white kernel; to set budding more
  And still more, later flowers for the bees,
  Until they think warm days will never cease
    For Summer has o'er brimm'd their clammy cells—

                        Who amid thy stores?
Who hath not seen thee? ~~for thy haunts are many~~
                        abroad
  Sometimes whoever seeks ~~for thee may~~ find
Thee sitting careless on a granary floor
  Thy hair soft lifted by the winnowing wind
    ~~While bright the sun slants through the~~ barn;
    ~~Or sound asleep in a half reaped field~~

      Dosed with read poppies, while thy ~~reaping~~ hook
~~Spares from some slumbers~~ warm slumbers creep
                ~~minutes while warm slumbers creep~~
Or on a half reap'd furrow sound asleep
  Dos'd with the fume of poppies, while thy hook
  ~~Spares the next swath and all its twined flowers~~
  ~~Spares for some slumberous minutes the next swath~~

    And sometimes like a gleaner thou dost keep
      Steady thy laden head across the brook;
      Or by a Cyder-press with patent look
        Thou watchest the last oozing hours by hours

Where are the songs of Sping? Aye where are they?
Think not of them thou hast thy music too –
      barred   bloom
While ~~a gold~~ cloud s ~~gilds~~ the soft-dying day
 and   with
~~And~~ Touch~~ing the~~ the stibble plains ^ rosy hue –
  Then in a waiful quire the small gnats mourn
    Among the river sallows, ~~on the~~ borne afots
    Or sinking as the light wind lives and dies;
*   Then full grown Lambs loud bleat from hilly bourn,
    Hedge crickets sing, and now agin full soft
     The Redbreast whistles from a garden croft
    ~~And now flock still~~
*   Then Gathering swallows twiter in the skies –

   *And   *And

Where are the songs of Spring? Aye, where are they?
    Think not of them Thou hast thy music too—
While a barred clouds bloom the soft dying day
    And Touching the the stubble plains with rosy hue—
Then in a wailful quire the small gnats mourn
    among the river sallows, borne aloft
        Or sinking as the light wind lives and dies;
And full grown lambs loud bleat from hilly bourn,
    Hedge crickets sing, and now again full soft
    The Redbreast whistles from a garden croft:
        And gathering swallows twitter in the Skies—

ON MELANCHOLY

No, No, go not to Lethe neither twist
~~Henb~~ Wolfsbane, tight rooted, for its poisonous
                                                               wine

Nor suffer thy pale forehead to be kist
  By Nightshade, ruby grape of Proserpine
  Make not your Rosary of yew berries
  Nor let the Beetle, or the death moth be
    Your mournful Psyche; nor the downy owl
A partner in your sorrows mysteries –
    For shade to sadade will come too ~~heavily~~
                            ~~too sleepily~~
                                drowsily

  And do^r^wn the wakeful anguish of the
                                 soul.

                            fall
But when the melanancholy fitt shall ~~come~~

                  a
  Sudden from heaven like weeping cloud
That fosters the droopheaded flowers all
  And hides the green hills in an april
                      shroud,
      glut
  Then ~~feed~~ thy sorrow on a morning rose
  Or on the rain-bow of the ~~dashing~~
                     salt sand wave
  Or on the wealth of globed Pionies
  Or if thy Mistress some rich anger shows
  Emprison her soft hand, and let her rave
  And feed deep deep upon her peerless eyes.

*shade

60

On Melancholy

No, No, go not to Lethe, neither twist
~~Wolfs~~ Wolfs bane, tight rooted, for its poisonous
                                                         wine
Nor suffer thy pale forehead to be kist.
By Night-shade, ruby grape of Proserpine
    Make not your Rosary of yew berries
        Nor let the Beetle, or the death moth be
I   Your mournful Psyche; nor the downy owl
    A partner in your sorrows mysteries.
        For shade to shade will come ~~to beauty~~
                                                         too drowsily
            And down the wakeful anguish ~~of the~~ drowning

But when the melancholy fit ~~shall~~ ~~fall~~
    Sudden from heaven like weeping cloud
    That fosters the droopheaded flowers all
    And hides the green hills in an april
        Then ~~feed~~ glut thy sorrow on a morning rose
        or on the rain-bow of the dashing
        Or on the wealth of globed Peonies
        Or if thy Mistress some rich anger shows
    Emprison her soft hand, and let her rave
    And feed deep deep upon her peerless eyes

She lives in Beauty — Beauty that must die
  And Joy whose hand is ever at his lips
Bidding Adieu: and aching Pleasure nigh
  Turning to Poison while the Bee-mouth sips
  Aye, in the very Temple of delight
  Veil'd Melancholy has her sovran shrine
                              him
    Though seen of none but ~~those~~ whose strenuous
                                        tongue
  Can burst joys grape against his palate fine
                  taste
    His soul shall the anguish of her might
  And be among her cloudy trophies hung

She lives in Beauty - Beauty that must die
And Joy whose hand is ever at his lips
Bidding Adieu; and aching Pleasure nigh
Turning to Poison while the Bee-mouth sips
Aye, in the very temple of delight .
    Veil'd Melancholy has her Sovran shrine
        Though seen of none but him whose ⟨⟩ memory
Can burst-joys grape against his palate fine
    His soul shall the anguish of her might
And be among her cloudy trophies hung

NOTES ON THE ODES AND THEIR
MANUSCRIPTS

Ode to a Nightingale

The composition of the *Ode to a Nightingale* appears at first sight to be the most fully documented act of poetic creation by Keats that we have; and, as such, the description of the event by Charles Brown, co-owner with Charles Wentworth Dilke of Wentworth Place, has almost always been accepted:

> In the spring of 1819 a nightingale had built her nest near my house. Keats felt a tranquil and continual joy in her song; and one morning he took his chair from the breakfast-table to the grass-plot under a plum-tree, where he sat for two or three hours. When he came into the house, I perceived he had some scraps of paper in his hand, and these he was quietly thrusting behind the books. On inquiry, I found these scraps, four or five in number, contained his poetic feeling on the song of our nightingale. The writing was not well legible; and it was difficult to arrange the stanzas on so many scraps. With his assistance I succeeded, and this was his *Ode to a Nightingale*, a poem which has been the delight of every one.

Monckton Milnes reproduced this account substantially in his biography of 1848; yet in his edition of Keats's poems in 1876, he completely removed Brown from the story, making Keats himself put together the 'scraps of paper' into the Ode. Something must have reached his ears of the scepticism of Dilke, who had dismissed Brown's Memoir of Keats as basically 'a dream on the subject'. In a draft letter to Severn, though not in the actual letter, Dilke had thrown extreme doubt on the accuracy of the 'Nightingale' story as 'a pure delusion', and in his copy of Milnes's 1848 volumes, he had allowed himself the sarcastic marginal annotation, 'We do not usually thrust waste paper behind books'.

Yet in spite of doubt and semi-retraction, the story has usually been accepted by those discussing the manuscript of Keats's first draft. That it is a first draft, which has sometimes also been doubted, is shown by the false start, 'Small, winged Dryad' on the second of the two half-sheets of note-paper on which the whole poem is written. That there are only two sheets — though written on both sides — would surely seem to throw doubt on Brown's whole story of 'four or five' scraps, which needed the care of himself and the poet to arrange. It may seem far more plausible to conjecture that Brown, writing twenty years after the event, liked to imagine that this incident concerned the Nightingale Ode, which had by then become famous; the probability is that it concerned the unpublished *Ode on Indolence*, whose holograph has disappeared, but of which the order of the stanzas has always been doubtful and often interchanged.

Brown's story may, however, have the sole value of showing the mood of concentration and the setting in which the Ode was written. The poem echoes closely a passage in a letter of 1 May 1819 from Keats to his sister Fanny, where he speaks of 'please heaven, a little claret-wine out of a cellar a mile deep ... a strawberry bed to say your prayers to Flora in'. It must therefore have been written very near May Day, and the order of the stanzas on the two half-sheets may well confirm a relaxed outdoor atmosphere. After the false start on sheet two, Keats wrote two and a half stanzas on sheet one. He then wrote the next two and a half on sheet two, turning it upside-down to avoid the false start. Stanzas six and seven were written on the verso of sheet one, and he then returned to the verso of sheet two to write stanza eight. These two small sheets, approximately eight by four and three quarter inches, have a history very closely related to that of the manuscript of the *Ode to Psyche*. Sent by Keats to J. H. Reynolds, possibly at the same time as the other ode, 4 May 1819, the two sheets passed to Reynolds's sisters, and eventually to the artist Towneley Green. After the death of the latter in 1900, it was bought by the Marquess of Crewe, who in 1933 gave it to the Fitzwilliam Museum, Cambridge.

Keats headed the poem quite deliberately 'Ode to the Nightingale', and it is likely that the substitution of 'a' for 'the' in the 1820 printing was made by his publishers. It does not appear in any manuscript, or in the *Annals of the Fine Arts* for July 1819, where the poem was also printed. The composition shows an increasing sureness of touch by Keats as the poem develops. Though 'Small, winged Dryad' suggests an actual glimpse of the bird, he abandoned this invocation for a more personal opening, not without difficulty, transferring at once the 'pains' of 'painful numbness' to make a more acceptable rhyme than 'falls'. The poem almost literally leaps forward from the seventh line, where the original vision reappears expanded as 'light-winged dryad of the trees'. There is hardly a falter in the whole second stanza, but it is worth noting that the 1820 'beaded bubbles' was, and remains here 'cluster'd bubbles', further evidence that this is the earliest manuscript. Alterations in the third stanza, especially in the section which, as Keats said himself, was associated with the death of his own brother Tom, seem largely concerned with avoiding echoes of Wordsworth's

While man grows old, and dwindles, and decays;

though this passage in *The Excursion* had such a hold on Keats that he returned to it unmistakably at the beginning of his own stanza seven. Stanza four caused more trouble, and two words which Keats had been overworking in his poems at that time, 'Cluster'd' and 'Sidelong', the latter reminiscent of *La Belle Dame Sans Merci*, had to be cancelled. With the latter, the line was adjusted by revision, but the cancellation of the former left the line incomplete. What had passed through Keats's mind was the realization that he had already used '*cluster'd* bubbles' in stanza two. The later invention of 'beaded' for the earlier image left 'cluster'd' free for use here, though he did not bother to amend his cancellation. Apart from a stumble over another over-worked word, 'blooms', and a kind of stammer in the

66

composition of the fourth line of stanza five, Keats shows a certainty and calm in this stanza that announces he is fully at home with the form and scope of this poem.

It was moreover becoming a longer and more substantial poem than Keats had anticipated when he had impulsively taken the two small sheets out into the garden. Fearing to break the continuity of what seemed more and more a fluent process of creation, he did not return to the house, but started the next stanzas on the back of his first sheet. These, however, had their difficulties, perhaps as continuous writing began to tire him. The adjective 'painless', banished in stanza one, came back into stanza six, and had to be altered, though unobserved here, to 'quiet'. The awkwardly coined 'requiem'd' was quickly removed from the last line of stanza six. In the intensely wrought stanza seven his difficulties increased. Accepting the returning echo of Wordsworth's

> And countless generations of mankind
> Depart, and leave no vestige where they trod

in his own opening lines, Keats made a minor alteration – 'song' for 'voice' in the fifth line – that may show, as Garrod has suggested, that the picture of Ruth is somehow connected with that of Wordsworth's Solitary Reaper, and the group-imagery of nightingale-voice-seas in that poem. The name of Ruth herself provided a stumbling-block in the final line of the stanza. Here Keats had in his mind the adjective 'ruthless' for the sea-image which recalled his own vision of the sea as a place of savage nature's destruction in his Lines to J. H. Reynolds a year before. This is proved by Richard Woodhouse's marginal shorthand note giving 'ruthless' as Keats's first version of the adjective 'perilous'. What Keats has obscured, in his hasty and heavy crossing out of the offending word, once he realised its cacophony with the 'Ruth' of the earlier line, is that his equally hasty hand originally wrote the meaningless word 'kuthless', the 'k' being quite distinct. This has led to a theory that he intended an even worse cacophony with 'keelless'; but the word, though badly erased, was certainly not that, and it was like Keats, in the heat of composition, to produce unknowingly a word not found in any dictionary as a kind of shorthand for himself. His 'afots' for 'aloft' in *To Autumn* is a striking example.

For his last stanza, turning to his only remaining spare bit of paper, the back of sheet two, Keats shows every sign of strain and effort, not only in the characteristic 'Folorn' for 'Forlorn', but in 'world' for 'word', both slips of the pen, incidentally, common in his swiftly written letters. The second line, muddled here, had to be revised before publication into a firmer form with 'sole self', as did the ninth, where the weak 'vision real' had its artificial inversion remedied. Keats, one may guess, was too exhausted by his unbroken hours of composing to do much at this late stage in the poem about the trap that the rhyming word 'self' had led him into, and 'elf', though echoed in turn in Wordsworth's Duddon sonnets, has been rightly criticized. Yet as a continuous feat of creation, this Ode is remarkable, and is perhaps justly his best-known and best-appreciated poem.

Ode on a Grecian Urn

The original manuscript in Keats's hand of his *Ode on a Grecian Urn* has disappeared. The last apparent mention of its whereabouts is in Keats's letter of 15 January 1820, when he is giving his sister-in-law in America the news about his brother George, who had returned to England to raise money. Writing to her, in the intensely cold weather of that winter, he remarked:

> George is busy this morning in making copies
> of my verses – He is making now one of an
> Ode to the nightingale, which is like reading
> an account of the b[l]ack hole at Calcutta
> on an ice bergh.

Since the *Ode on a Grecian Urn* appears in George's handwriting immediately after his transcript of the *Ode to a Nightingale*, it is to be presumed that he went on to copy it the same morning. It is also to be presumed that he copied it from Keats's original first draft, since this is certainly so with his other copies taken at this time, notably *To Autumn*.

George Keats's copy, reproduced here, is therefore the nearest to Keats's first draft that we are likely to get. This copy has had a curious history. George had been absent from England for about eighteen months, during which Keats had written many of his greatest poems, including all the Odes. Of these, he had sent the *Ode to Psyche*, copied into a letter, to George, but the others were unknown to his brother, who proceeded to make copies of these and other newly written poems, notably *The Eve of St Agnes*. Keats gave him for this purpose a small leather-bound octavo note-book, measuring approximately seven inches by four and a half. This was a working poetry note-book of Keats's own. In it he himself had fair-copied the whole of *Isabella, or The Pot of Basil* and the lines beginning 'Souls of poets dead and gone'. He had also used it for the first draft of the unfinished *The Eve of St Mark*, which he had written in it sometime between 13 and 17 February 1819, a few months before composing the Odes. His object in giving George the note-book seems to have been that his brother would not need to copy the poems already in it, but would add himself other poems, such as all the Odes except *Psyche* which he already had. George copied *The Eve of St Agnes* and then immediately proceeded to copy the remaining Odes, with the exception of *To Autumn*, which he added after copying two other poems. He then took the note-book back to America, together with some of the originals, though not, apparently, that of the *Ode on a Grecian Urn*.

The history of this remarkable little volume, containing fair-copies and original work by the poet, and copies of this work by his brother, then becomes obscure; but it seems to have stayed in the possession of George's family until at least 1880. There is a very strongly held tradition among the descendants of George Keats that when George's grandson, John Gilmer Speed, produced his three-volume

The Letters and Poems of John Keats in 1883, he took, for his own disposal, a great deal of Keats material which never returned to the rest of the family. This may well account for the undoubted fact that early in 1891, the note-book appeared in Melbourne, Australia, where it was bought by Edward Jenks, Professor of Law to the University of Melbourne. Jenks wrote a descriptive article, dated 29 March 1891, and printed in *The Athenæum* of 23 May 1891, pages 667–8. He rightly conjectured that the book had been taken by George to America in 1820, but offered no clue how it had reached Melbourne; nor did he identify the handwriting in it. His article was probably merely to arouse interested purchasers; for within two years, the book was in the hands of Bernard Quaritch, who sold it to the British Museum on 11 April 1893. It was bought from the Farnborough Fund, and is Egerton Ms. 2780. Its description in the *Catalogue of Additions to the Manuscripts in the British Museum* 1888–93, pp. 472–3, contains several misleading and confused statements.

Without Keats's first draft, little can be said about his actual detailed process of composition. The copy he evidently made for James Elmes to print in *Annals of the Fine Arts*, No. XV, of January 1820 has similarly disappeared, though it can be inferred that he made his usual crop of fair-copy mistakes. It is extremely likely that the curious printed half-line in stanza two, 'bid the spring adieu' instead of 'can those trees be bare', which completely destroys the rhyme, was an aberration on Keats's part, perhaps suggested by the similar expression in the third stanza, or a mere printer's error. The variations in the 1820 volume of poems, however, were almost certainly, like many other innovations in that publication, the work of Keats's publishers, and may profitably be compared with George's transcript, which gives more or less what his brother would seem to have wished.

It is also interesting to examine at the same time the general inspiration and formation of this Ode. It obviously leans heavily for its ideas and for some of its expressions on two magazine articles printed on 2 and 9 May 1819, and was therefore written about the middle of that month. This, and its maturity of expression and sure handling of form, may possibly date it as the last of this sequence of summer odes. The two articles were written in *The Examiner*, which Keats read weekly, by B. R. Haydon, and they discuss Raphael's cartoon, *The Sacrifice at Lystra*. They do not mention urns, and indeed, it has been shown that Keats's urn is a hybrid, not descriptive of any single one, but taken from features of several he had probably seen in the print-books of Haydon's studio. His first stanza is therefore a very generalized picture of the Greek scenes depicted, and little more need be said about it, except that Keats's publishers seem to have objected to the rather exclamatory 'What love? what dance?' of line nine, and substituted for publication the equally unsatisfactory 'What mad pursuit?'.

The next three stanzas develop the main theme of the poem, that of the eternal quality of art when compared with human experience. This was no new theme for Keats; long before he had expounded to the artist Joseph Severn his ideas about the spirit of Greek life and art. It was, he said, 'an eternal youth'; there was 'no

Now or *Then*' for it, any more than there would be for the Holy Ghost. Yet the concrete expression of these values, recently read in the articles by another artist, Haydon, were imported unmistakably into these stanzas of Keats's poem. The garlanded heifer, the priest and worshippers, the town emptied of its inhabitants to attend sacrifice, even the player on the sylvan pipes, whom Haydon described as 'wholly absorbed in the harmony of his own music', all appear in the articles, transmuted into the form of the Ode with very little essential change. Even the central theme of the agelessness of art was put in almost the same words by Haydon, who, passing to the classical statuary creations of Michelangelo, remarked that they 'look as if they were above the influence of time; they seem as if they would never grow old, and had never been young'. It seems that Keats's publishers recognized that here was a tone of voice moulded to the poet's thoughts, even if the expression was borrowed; for their sole alterations for publication show a more sympathetic understanding of his purpose than usual. The substitution of 'yet' for 'O' in line eighteen corrects a slight sensation of weakness, while one other change probably made by them, 'flanks' for 'sides' in stanza four, positively enhances the picture and heightens its resemblance to two other pervasive influences on Keats, the Elgin Marbles, and the landscapes of Claude Lorrain.

Their deviation from what George had copied in the final stanza — and, indeed, from all transcripts of this verse — was not so happy, and may be said to have confused the meaning of the poem for generations. In the last two lines, his publishers put the words 'Beauty is truth, truth beauty' in quotation-marks. This made these five words only an utterance by the Urn, and the remainder of the last two lines a comment by the poet. It has been shown, on the evidence of this transcript by George, and all others, that the whole of the last two lines is a summary of its message by the Urn. Even then, the interpretations are many, and continue to be made; but, on the evidence of this earliest version, the poet, true to his own often-expressed philosophy, has withdrawn himself, and attempted no excursion into the type of didactic utterance he himself condemned in the poetry of others. The Urn indeed puts forward an interpretation of human life often canvassed by Keats in his letters; but he himself, with the philosophic questionings of human fate that run through all the Odes, will not set himself up to provide any final answer.

Ode to Psyche

Keats drafted the *Ode to Psyche* on a single sheet of the white wove paper known as 'Bath', that is a large size of note-paper, eight by fourteen inches when flat, and folding into four pages of approximately eight by seven. It was a paper which he himself described in his letters as used by 'Boarding schools and suburbans in general', and though he employed it often for his own letters, it may reflect here the extra care he thought he was taking over this poem. On 4 May 1819, he gave this draft to his friend J. H. Reynolds, who kept it until his own death in 1852. Reynolds appears to have let it out of his sight only twice, once to Richard Woodhouse, who made a copy of it at some unspecified date, and, years later on 2 July 1847, to Richard Monckton Milnes for the preparation of his Keats biography. On Reynolds's death, it passed to his sisters, of whom the youngest, Charlotte, died in 1884. On her death she willed it to her nephew, the artist Towneley Green. After the death of the latter, it came up for sale at Sotheby's in 1901, when it was sold for eighty-six pounds. It then disappeared for over half a dozen years, until in 1909 it was acquired by the Pierpont Morgan Library from an unknown source.

Keats, as has been said, claimed to be taking special pains with this draft. 'This I have done leisurely,' he announced, 'I think it reads the more richly for it and will I hope encourage me to write other thing[s] in even a more peacable and healthy spirit'. It may therefore seem a contradiction that no corrections occur in this manuscript until lines thirteen and fourteen. Yet it is most significant that they should occur at this precise place. It seems clear that Keats, up to this point, thought he was writing yet another sonnet, of which he had 'dashed off', as he said, several in the third week in April. It is plain from this manuscript that Keats had first entitled these fourteen lines 'To Psyche'; the word 'Ode' is added away to the left and at a different angle. It is just, then, where these first minor corrections creep in that the poem ceased to be a sonnet and becomes the first of the Odes. Line fourteen, where this happens, is also a curious battlefield of interpretations. Keats pencilled the compound adjective 'freckle-pink' in its margin, as a substitute for his other compound 'silver-white'; this is probably what he meant to print, since he used it uncompromisingly in the version he copied for his brother, the day before giving the original manuscript to Reynolds. He also used in both these versions the expression 'budded syrian', so that the line he intended read

> Blue, freckle-pink, and budded syrian,

His publishers, making up the copy in 1820, and given virtually a free hand by Keats's severe illness, were puzzled by the line. No one to this day knows quite what Keats may have meant by 'syrian'. Their solution was to invent an intelligible compromise. They restored 'silver-white', Richard Woodhouse pencilling it back in the copy he had taken from Reynolds's, but kept Keats's effort to introduce colour into the line by altering the obscure 'syrian' to the conventional

'Tyrian', suggesting the traditional purple dye. As appears by their alterations to other poems, the publishers' chief object was to placate critics by dodging any suggestion of the quaintness and coining of words, for which *Endymion* was attacked, and their doctoring of this fourteenth line was the result. Similarly, it was almost certainly they (and not Keats himself, as H. W. Garrod has it) who, alarmed by the odd word 'fan' ending line ten, substituted the synonym 'roof', but failed to see they had destroyed the sonnet-rhymes by doing so.

Unconscious of this future tinkering, Keats now went on to develop his sonnet-beginning into an ode. He himself failed to notice that the next line, number fifteen, was left for ever and in the printed edition without a rhyme; but he achieved a first stanza of twenty-three lines confidently, with only one alteration, 'eye-dawn' for 'dawning', to complete his picture of the embracing Cupid and Psyche, so like one of his own favourite passages from Milton, the bower of Adam and Eve. He then turned to elaborate, in the new expansion of the poem's form, what was to be its main theme: again, as he explained to his brother George

> You must recollect that Psyche was not embodied as a goddess before the time of Apulieus the Platonist who lived after the Agustan age, and consequently the Goddess was never worshipped or sacrificed to with any of the ancient fervour – and perhaps never thought of in the old religion – I am more orthodox that (*for* than) to let a hethen Goddess be so neglected –

In other words, he would show himself in this poem to be the Priest of the Soul, as he had sketched in his philosophy of Soul-making a few days earlier. The next stanza therefore cost him some difficulty, though, once he got going, the memory of Milton again helped him out. His chief hold-up was over the fine expression 'Phoebe's sapphire-region'd star', which came partly from a favourite line of his in *Comus*; while his actual description of a pagan priest, his 'pale-mouth'd Prophet dreaming' had certain affinity with 'the pale-ey'd Priest' of Milton's *On the Morning of Christ's Nativity*. This stanza stayed as it was from draft to publication, apart from an unfortunate weak substitution – 'delicious' for 'melodious' – which he himself inserted in the thirtieth line.

The next and companion stanza, with its returning refrain, also stayed more or less the same from draft to publication, apart from an improvement almost certainly made by his publishers. Keats plunged into it with one of his least happy evocations – 'O Bloomiest' – and was satisfied enough to let it stand in all versions. To his publishers, however, it was all too reminiscent of the lush exaggerations of style they themselves had disliked in *Endymion*, and they provided the colourless but inoffensive 'brightest'. Keats's own second thoughts are unimportant – 'among' for 'above' in line forty-two, 'own' instead of 'clear' in the next line – but he evidently felt some unease that the line 'Upon the midnight hours' was left without a rhyme. It was, true, in the section repeated from the previous stanza where it was similarly unrhymed; but in his feeling toward the new ode-form, he seems to have worried that it might be too irregular. Accordingly, he wrote at right-angles down the left-hand margin a tentative rhyming line, 'Thy

Altar heap'd with flowers,'; but this seemed to exaggerate the many attributes of the Goddess's temple, and he quickly drove two pen-strokes through it.

His stage was now set for the final stanza where he presented himself as Psyche's poetic priest. The scene was to be

In some untrodden Region of my mind

but physically it was taken not only from the translation of Apuleius he had been reading in William Adlington's 1566 version, but also from the garden setting of Wentworth Place and his close proximity to his neighbour Fanny Brawne. The alterations he makes in the later lines of this stanza have a tangible firmness that hints at a real situation. He himself is not merely a worshipping priest but also Cupid, waiting for the opening casement 'To let the warm Love in', his inspired re-writing of the concluding line, which like the rest of the stanza stayed fixed in the final printing.

'Here endethe ye Ode to Psyche', wrote Keats with deceptive playfulness as he finished copying (not without hasty mistakes) in his letter to George. Looking through this comparatively unscored first draft, so close to the published version, we may question Keats's claim that this poem was 'the first and the only one with which I have taken even moderate pains'. Yet we do not know all the unwritten changes that went on in his mind; and we can see that one of them was a major and even revolutionary step: to alter and expand what started as a perfectly good and self-contained sonnet 'To Psyche' into the much larger conception of an Ode. That this would lead in turn to the greater ode-sequence, in which it now stands as a prologue, was probably only dimly apprehended by Keats, if at all at this point. Yet something of the feeling that a new era was opening in his own poetry surely contributed to his attitude over this Ode. He regarded it as a stepping-stone to 'encourage me to write other thing[s]'. The achievement of these other works should not lead us to undervalue the effort he put into the composition of their predecessor.

To Autumn

The history of the first draft of Keats's *To Autumn* is a remarkably straightforward one; it displays none of the vicissitudes to which many of his other manuscripts were subjected. He composed it on a large sheet of paper, approximately $7\frac{3}{4}$ by $10\frac{3}{4}$ inches on Sunday, 19 September 1819, making a fair copy, as usual not without mistakes, for Richard Woodhouse two days later. It was from this fair copy, with 'ripeness' for 'sweetness' in the sixth line, that the text in the 1820 volume was evidently set up. The first draft seems to have stayed in Keats's possession until the visit from America of his brother George in January 1820. George employed some of his time during this visit in copying his brother's poems into the note-book which he took back with him to America. Usually, he seems not to have taken with him the manuscript from which he copied; but, together with the *Ode on Melancholy*, he made an exception with *To Autumn*. He not only copied this from Keats's first draft – his copying 'sweetness' instead of 'ripeness' proves this – but he took the actual first draft with him. There is no question of it reaching him after Keats's death; he himself complained that he had been sent no relics of his brother, and Dilke, writing to Severn twenty years after Keats's death, was explicit that George had received 'not so much as an old volume or refuse sheet that had belonged to his brother'.

The draft manuscript then remained in the hands of George Keats at Louisville, Kentucky, until 15 November 1839. In that month, George was introduced by his close friend, James Freeman Clarke, to a young woman from New Orleans, Miss Anna H. Barker. She had already made a favourable impression on George's daughter Emma Frances; but what strongly endeared her to George was that she had gathered and preserved flowers from Keats's grave in Rome, one of which she presented to him. Touched by this, and moved by the impulsive generosity that was part of the Keats temperament, George wrote her a short note enclosing as a return present the manuscript of *To Autumn*, for her to 'value highly and treasure carefully'. Miss Barker, who married Samuel Gray Ward of Boston in the following year, kept the manuscript for over fifty years, and inscribed it to her grand-daughter, Elizabeth Ward (afterwards Perkins), on 14 May 1896. From Mrs Perkins it passed in 1921 to Miss Amy Lowell, who bequeathed it to the Harvard College Library in 1925.

The circumstances under which Keats composed *To Autumn* are equally clear. In September 1819 he was staying in Winchester, at first accompanied by Charles Brown, but then on his own. He had just finished the play *Otho the Great* and the narrative poem *Lamia*, and was attempting to recast *Hyperion* into a more personal vision, reading Dante's Inferno in the process, and also reviving his early love of Chatterton's poems. While he was engaged on this, on Friday, 10 September, he received a letter from George in America appealing urgently for financial help. Keats at once took coach for London, bundling up his unpublished poems with

74

the idea that they should be printed immediately; he also planned to obtain money from his ex-guardian out of the undistributed estate of his dead brother Tom. After a long but inconclusive week-end, during which both publisher and guardian were tactful but unforthcoming, Keats returned to Winchester on Wednesday, 15 September. Recalled into the poetic mood of the earlier odes which he had collected together, and whose traces appear in the revised *Hyperion*, thrown back into the fruitful state of composition which his brother's dilemma had interrupted, Keats also resumed his enjoyment of the countryside near Winchester, in which he walked every day. On Tuesday, 21 September he wrote to J. H. Reynolds

> How beautiful the season is now – How fine the air. A temperate sharpness about it. Really, without joking, chaste weather – Dian skies – I never lik'd stubble fields so much as now – Aye better than the chilly green of the spring. Somehow a stubble plain looks warm – in the same way that some pictures look warm – this struck me so much in my sunday's walk that I composed upon it.

The influences leading him to write *To Autumn* are plain. First there was the season itself and his surroundings, described in the letter which borrows actual phrases from the poem. Then, his re-reading of the summer odes brought him back to their form which he had neglected for drama and narrative. Poetically, the clear objective statement of Dante's brief similes, which he was enjoying both in the original Italian and in Cary's translation, mingled happily in his mind with the simplicities of Chatterton, whom he considered at this exact time to be 'the purest writer in the English Language'. Moreover, the troubles and storms of the previous week had led him to value a calm which he hoped to import into his poetry – 'a more thoughtful and quiet power'. The opening stanza, strengthened by adding an extra line, but otherwise in the form of the summer odes, has this serenity. The vines, originally in a more prominent part of line four, remind one of Dante. The 'white kernel' of line eight gains its adjective from the autumnal song in Chatterton's *Aella*, and there is an even stronger parallel between Chatterton's

> When the fair apple, red as even sky,
> Do bend the tree unto the fruitful ground,

and Keats's hastily written

> To bend with apples the moss'd cottage trees
> And fill all furuits with sweeness to the core

The 'white' kernel inevitably went when the earlier change to 'ripeness' left the adjective 'sweet' available, but on the whole this first stanza was printed very much as first drafted, and reflects how very successfully Keats assimilated these varied influences, both personal and literary.

The second stanza shows more difficulty, as Keats tried to personify Autumn by a series of pictures, as he had personified so memorably the figures of Beauty, Joy and Pleasure in the final stanza of the *Ode on Melancholy*. Twice, his first thoughts led him into rhymes that could not be supported, and forced him to

75

revise the lines in which they occurred. Both 'many' and 'swath' (lines 12 and 18 of the poem) were end-rhymes which would have caused impossible and even comic poetic situations. His alterations here are all dictated by the need for easier rhyming words; but his long hesitations over lines fifteen and sixteen came from the wish to present a complete and vivid picture of the figure of Autumn. These revisions all move away from the slack and conventional adjective-noun combination – 'red poppies', 'slumbrous minutes', 'warm slumbers' – to a sharper and less adorned style, in which, like Dante again, the object is brought simply into the foreground. His final hesitations over 'Dos'd' and 'Dased' (which he substituted in the copy to Woodhouse, but may not entirely have meant) were resolved on printing by his publishers; they, once more anxious to avoid any critical attack for quaintness, plumped for the conventional though less interesting 'Drows'd'.

The third stanza was composed at white heat; some of the spellings – as 'afots' for 'aloft' – are merely notations to remind him what he meant as he pressed on. He is intent to make a set of personal impressions catch the philosophic mood in which he found himself. He repeats some of them almost precisely in his prose letter two days later. In this effort, he tries everywhere to speak with his own voice, and to shake off any reminiscence of any other poet. The third line of the stanza

> While a gold cloud gilds the soft dying day

was at once rejected because of its close resemblance to another line in Chatterton's *Aella*, which, according to Leigh Hunt, was always a favourite with Keats –

> With his gold hand gilding the falling leaf

The last lines of all cost him some pains, as he strove to give final perfection to a series of simple objective pictures drawn from nature, in which the method of Dante is transmuted into Keats's own real experiences. Only the 'small gnats' are taken direct from Dante; others remind one of the telling bird-images of Dante's Canto Five. The calling cranes and the massed starlings of this canto, much-read by Keats, become his whistling redbreast and the gathering swallows. Like Dante, Keats gives by these small touches a sense of eternity, unspoken but implicit. One improvement, 'with treble soft', was made by Keats a day later. For the rest, this stanza, swiftly written but with his new 'quiet power', was hardly altered from its original draft.

Ode on Melancholy

It seems likely that we do not have the first and original draft of Keats's *Ode on Melancholy*. Its very first draft had, according to Charles Brown and to Richard Woodhouse apparently on Brown's information, this rejected opening stanza, much in the style of some of Keats's favourite reading, Robert Burton's *The Anatomy of Melancholy* and Dante's Inferno in Cary's version:

> Though you should build a bark of dead men's bones,
>   And rear a phantom gibbet for a mast,
> Stitch creeds together for a sail, with groans
>   To fill it out, blood-stained and aghast;
> Although your rudder be a dragon's tail
>   Long sever'd, yet still hard with agony,
>   Your cordage large uprootings from the skull
> Of bald Medusa, certes you would fail
>   To find the Melancholy – whether she
>   Dreameth in any isle of Lethe dull.

No draft that we have shows this cancelled opening. It seems likely, then, that the two pages we now have in Keats's handwriting were a second draft or revised copy. This is suggested by the regular spacing and indenting of the lines. This revised copy, however, did not finally satisfy Keats, and he made changes on it which altered the poem, though in seemingly minor ways, with a very considerable and major set of improvements.

The two sheets, or rather half-sheets of notepaper, on which he did this, seem to have become separated sometime in Keats's lifetime. Sheet one, containing the first two stanzas of the Ode, were taken by his brother George Keats to America early in 1820. George valued all his brother's manuscripts, but like his brother he had sudden impulses. One of these seems to have led him to give the sheet, sometime about 1837, to John Howard Payne, the American actor, playwright and lyricist of 'Home, Sweet Home'. Payne ended his days as a minor diplomat, and at his death in 1852, the sheet passed to Robert Smith Chilton, a young consular secretary, who wrote the verses on Payne's tomb. In 1897, when Smith was U.S. Consul in Ontario, the manuscript was still in his possession, and was noticed in a collection of essays by T. W. Higginson entitled *Book and Heart*. A few years later it was in the possession of Alfred T. White, who willed it to his daughter Mrs Adrian Van Sinderen. She gave it to her son, Alfred W. Van Sinderen, who recently sold it to Robert H. Taylor of Princeton, New Jersey. It is the only portion of a Keats ode not in a public collection.

The second sheet, with only the third and last stanza, had an eventful and uncertain history. It seems to have been salvaged from Keats's effects by Charles Brown. Brown lived at Plymouth from 1835 to 1841, and made friends in the local literary society, to which he belonged. One of his closest allies there was

Colonel Charles Hamilton Smith. Sometime before 1841, when Brown emigrated to New Zealand, he gave this sheet to the Colonel's sister, Miss Hamilton Smith. From her it passed to her nephew (or perhaps niece) S. T. Whiteford, possibly in the late 1870s. A considerable space of unrecorded history then occurs, until on 25 July 1932 (not 1931 as H. W. Garrod has it) the sheet was sold by Sotheby's on behalf of Captain J. S. (later Sir James Stuart) Coats. It eventually passed into the collection of W. T. N. Howe of Cincinnati, which in 1940 was bought en bloc by the Berg Collection of the New York Public Library, where the sheet now is.

To return to the first sheet, containing stanzas one and two of the published poem, it is clear that their abrupt opening owes something to the fact that Keats is answering his own cancelled stanza, with its grotesque list of the conventional symbols of Melancholy, adapted from Burton's very similar catalogues of symptoms. The crossed-out 'Henbane' is itself taken from Burton's list of remedies for what he called Head-Melancholy. Keats let the rest of the stanza stand until he came to the last line but one, with its somewhat weak rhyme in '-y'. He did not do anything radical, such as altering the rhyme, but he tried 'heavily' and 'sleepily', before settling for 'drowsily'.

The beginning of the next stanza provides something of a puzzle. The manuscript presents, as has been said, all the appearance of a first fair copy on which Keats added a few corrections. Why then, is the rhyming word of the first line altered? The answer seems to be that Keats was specially distracted while copying out that line, and made a number of mistakes, as he often did when copying hastily, including the wrong rhyming word 'come' instead of 'fall'. His extraordinary spelling of 'melancholy fit' in this line lends plausibility to the idea that his mind was not on what he was doing at this point. He plainly, however, meant 'hills' and not 'hill' in line four, and the putting of the word in the singular must be attributed to his publishers for the 1820 edition, the only place where it occurs. He found weaknesses in the next two lines, five and six of this stanza, which on second thoughts he saw that he could improve considerably. They read

Then feed thy sorrow on a morning rose
Or on the rain-bow of the dashing wave

and they certainly had some relation with Keats's lines to J. H. Reynolds, written a year before and echoed in two other odes, *Grecian Urn* and *Nightingale*. Keats remembered his lines

the wide sea did weave
An untumultuous fringe of silver foam
Along the flat brown sand

and used them, though not explicitly, to strengthen his pictures of the externals of life, here as in the Reynolds lines serving as symbols of Melancholy and Destruction. He achieved, in much firmer and stronger language

Then glut thy sorrow on a morning rose
Or on the rain-bow of the salt sand wave

and so eliminated the weaker and more conventional epithets.

78

An even more important intention by Keats can be seen in the line

Or if thy Mistress some rich anger shows

which has always been printed with a small 'm' for 'mistress', but appears here with a capital. This and its following lines have been accused of masochism, sadism – though surely very mild – and, what is perhaps worse, of painting a rather silly and 'Cockney' picture of the young poet flirtatiously holding on to his girl-friend's wrists while she struggles to get away. None of this is necessary if we read, as apparently the poet intended, 'Mistress' with a capital. She then becomes the personification of Melancholy itself; and indeed this squares exactly with the cancelled first stanza. There 'the Melancholy' is addressed openly as a person, and the word 'she' clearly refers to her alone. What Keats is saying, strongly allied with the philosophy he found on this point in Burton, is that Melancholy itself is a desirable experience, and far from trying to reject it, the sufferer should seize on to its manifestations and make out of them a new and peculiar strength.

This idea is carried out logically and completely in the final stanza, where the 'She' is openly the personified figure of Melancholy, and appears with other personifications, Beauty, Joy, Pleasure and Delight. Keats noticed little to alter here, except to change the awkward tongue-twister of 'those whose' into the simple and easy 'him whose'. He failed to notice, however, in the first line of the stanza, that he had a distinct echo of another poet, Byron's lyric 'She walks in beauty, like the night'. His publishers altered 'She lives in Beauty' to 'She dwells with Beauty', almost certainly to avoid this echo in the final printed version. They also got him to make, before this version was set up, an alteration in the last line but one, where Keats had neglected to see how he was echoing his own earlier stanza.

His soul shall taste the anguish of her might

was far too like the closing line of stanza one –

And drown the wakeful anguish of the soul.

Keats got out of this by substituting the not altogether convincing 'sadness' in the later line; but, on the whole, the few improvements dotted throughout the manuscript, as we have it here, do add to its strength, and save it from the accusation, still sometimes made, of a lush and Romantic weakness. Though one may not see it entirely, as John Middleton Murry did, as a poem of triumph through despair, yet Keats's revisions on this manuscript distinctly confirm a movement in his mind towards a philosophy of stoic acceptance; they give it a place, in the whole process of the Odes, in the progress toward the final resignation and resolution of the summing-up he attempted in *To Autumn*.